Farming

Ruth Thomson

W

FRANKLIN WATTS
LONDON•SYDNEY

Note for parents and teachers

The Changing Times series is soundly based on the requirements of the History Curriculum. Using the device of four generations of a real family, the author combines reminiscences of this family with other people's oral evidence. The oral history is matched with photographs and other contemporary sources. Many other lessons are hidden in the text, which practises the skills of chronological sequencing, gives reference to a timeline and introduces the language and vocabulary of the past. Young children will find much useful information here, as well as a new understanding of the recent history of everyday situations and familiar things.

This edition 2004

Franklin Watts
96 Leonard Street
London EC2A 4XD

Franklin Watts Australia
45–51 Huntley Street
Alexandria
NSW 2015

Copyright © 1994 Franklin Watts

Editor: Sarah Ridley
Designer: Michael Leaman
Photographer: Peter Millard
Picture researcher: Sarah Moule

A CIP catalogue record for this book is available from the British Library.
Dewey Decimal Classification Number: 394.2

ISBN 0 7496 5251 9

Acknowledgements: The author and publishers would like to thank the following people and organisations for their help with the preparation of this book: Jenny, Teifi, Aled and Rhiannon Davies, Ernys and Rachel Davies, George and Molly Shore, Alice Shore, Amy Merrill, Janet Fleming, William Short of the Ffynnonwen Farm Museum, Anne Rogers of *Farmers Weekly*.

Printed in Malaysia

Contents

My name is Aled.
I was born in 1987.
I have one sister, called Rhiannon.
She is younger than me.

4-9

My name is Jenny.
I am Aled's mother.
I was born in 1956.

10-15

My name is George.
I am Jenny's father
and Aled's grandfather.
I was born in 1933.

16-23

My name is Alice.
I am George's mother,
Jenny's grandmother
and Aled's great-grandmother.
I was born in 1911.

24-29

Things to do   30-31

Index   32

I live on a farm.

We have a small herd of cows.
Sometimes I help Dad
round them up for milking.

Dad milks the cows
twice a day.

The milk is piped into a big refrigerated vat.
A milk tanker comes every morning to collect it.

After the cows have been milked,
we sweep the yard.

We feed the calves
in the calf shed.
They are too young
to graze in the fields.

I help Dad change
their straw bedding.

Dad grows grass
for the cows to eat.
He cuts it with a mower
to make into silage
for winter feed.

The big bales of silage
are stacked until he needs them.

We grow all sorts of vegetables, herbs and flowers.

Dad plants potatoes in the fields.

Mum grows marrows
and pumpkins
under plastic.

She grows beans, onions
and carrots in our garden.

She pickles some of the onions
and beetroot.

Mum sells the vegetables and pickles in our farm shop.

Other farmers nearby make cheese, cream and yogurt. We sell these in our shop, too.

Mum lived on a farm when she was young.
I asked her what it was like.

She said,

'We had about 60 cows and a bull.
In summer, the cows lived in the fields.
In winter, they were kept inside.'

'We took the calves
away from the mothers
and fed them ourselves.
One of my jobs was mixing
milk powder for them.'

'The cows were milked by machine.'

'The milk was put in big churns for a milk lorry to collect every day.'

'One year, there was an outbreak of foot and mouth disease. Even if only one cow on the farm got it, then they all had to be killed.'

Mum's family grew corn and hay for their cattle to eat.

She said,

'In spring, Dad ploughed the fields and sowed the seeds.'

'When the corn was ripe,
it was cut with a combine.
Two men bagged up the corn
and dropped it on to the ground.'

'A tractor and trailer picked up the sacks
and took them to the granary loft to dry.'

I asked Mum what else happened on her farm.

She said,

'We had chickens.
When I was young,
they roamed around
and laid their eggs in the fields.
We used to go and look for them.'

'When I was older,
Dad kept chickens
in a battery house.
It was dark, smelly and noisy.'

'Dad had a lot of farm machines.
All the greasing and sharpening
of the mower and combine knives
was done by hand.
That took up a lot of time.'

Oil can

'We weren't allowed
to help much.
There were too many
dangerous machines.
We did help by feeding
and cleaning out the animals.'

'My sister and I
both had ponies.
We spent hours
riding around
the fields and
making jumps.'

Grandad was brought up on the farm
where he still lives.
I asked him what it was like when he was young.

He said,

'We kept a few of everything –
cows, pigs, chickens, ducks
and geese.'

'The pigs lived in little huts in the fields.
We fed them on corn, carrots and potatoes.
We sold them at an auction
when they were a few months old.'

'There was an incubator
in the front room
to keep hen eggs warm.
We turned them every day by hand
until the chicks hatched.'

'We hatched day-old turkeys
to fatten them for Christmas.'

Grandad said,

'We had three shire horses.'

'In winter time, one pulled a cart
full of manure around the fields.
We put the manure in heaps
and spread it with a long-handled fork.'

'In spring time, we guided the horses up and down
the fields, with a plough or harrow.'

'In summer time, they pulled the binder which cut the corn and tied it into sheaves.'

'The sheaves were stood in upright stooks to dry. Then we loaded them on to a cart and took them back to the farmyard.'

'At mealtimes we brought food for the harvesters. Mother brought big jugs of hot tea.'

'In the autumn, a threshing machine came to thresh the corn. It travelled from farm to farm.'

1975

1950

Grandad said,

'The Second World War started
when I was six.
The government asked farmers
to grow as much food as possible.'

'Farmers near us were told
to grow a lot of potatoes.'

HOLIDAYS...
HARVEST DAYS...
HAPPY DAYS...

BRING IN THE
VICTORY HARVESTS
OCTOBER · · · MID-AUGUST & SEPTEMBER · · · END JULY-EARLY AUG
or
POTATOES · GRAIN · FRUIT

'I spent weeks and weeks going from farm to farm
to pick them by hand.'

'Lots of women came to help on farms, because so many men went away to fight. Everyone called them land girls.'

1975   1950

Grandad said,

'We didn't have to buy much food.
We grew or made it ourselves.'

Butter churn

'Mother made our butter.
She put soured cream into a glass churn.
She turned the handle
until the cream turned to butter.'

Butter pats

Butter
stamp

Butter mould

'She lifted the butter out
with wooden butter pats
and patted it into an oblong.'

'Some people stamped patterns into
the butter using a wooden mould.'

22

1925   1900

'Our farm was very go-ahead.
We were one of the
first local farms to milk
our cows by machine.'

'When I was eight, father
bought our first tractor.
But most of the other farms
around us still used horses
to pull machinery.'

1975   1950

I asked Great-grandma about the farm
where she lived when she was young.

She said,

'It was only a small farm.
Mother and Father did
all the work themselves.
All the children had jobs as well.'

Milking
stool

'My mother milked the cows by hand.
She sat on a stool under the cow.
The milk went into a bucket.'

Churn

'The milk was poured through a sieve into a big churn.'

Sieve

Milk measures

'We took the churn to a dairy by cart.
We sold some of the milk in nearby villages.
We measured it out in pint and quart pots.'

I asked Great-grandma what machines
there were on the farm.

She said,

'There were no tractors or cars then.
We had a horse, called Doll,
to pull the machines and the carts.'

'At haymaking time, she pulled a mower
which cut the hay.'

'Our neighbours grew corn.'

'A travelling threshing machine came
to thresh their corn after the harvest.
That was a dusty, dirty, tiring job.'

1975   1950

I asked Great-grandma
about the food her family grew.

She said,

'We grew all our own vegetables.
We sold whatever we didn't need
at the local market.'

'We grew swedes
to feed to our animals.'

'We had a small orchard
with apples, plums and damsons.
We made jams with them.
We stored the apples on straw
in a dark shed over the winter.'

'Once a year, a man who worked
for the butcher came to kill a pig for us.
He put it in boiling water,
so he could scrape off the bristles.'

'Nothing was wasted.
We boiled up the head.
We made sausages.
The boys blew up
the bladder as a football.'

Things to do

Aled's family grows these vegetables,
flowers and herbs.
Do you know all their names?

End-over-end butter churn

These things were found on farms in your great-grandparents' childhood. What were they used for?

Cream scoop

Nosebag

Milk churn

Butter mould

Hay knife

Index

Binder 19
butter 22
butter churn 22, 31

Calves 6, 10
cart 18, 19, 25, 26
chickens 14, 16
churn 11, 22, 25, 31
combine 13, 15
corn 12, 13, 16, 19, 27
cows 4, 5, 7, 10, 11, 16, 23, 24

Eggs 14, 17

Farm shop 9
field 6, 8, 10, 12, 14, 15, 16, 18
foot and mouth disease 11

Hay 12, 26

horses 18, 23, 26

Land girls 21

Manure 18
milk 5, 10, 11, 23, 24, 25
mower 7, 15, 26

Orchard 28

Pigs 16, 29
potatoes 8, 16, 20

Second World War 20-21
silage 7

Threshing machine 19, 27
tractor 13, 23, 26
turkeys 17, 27

Photographs: Barnabys Picture Library cover bl, 13b, 15tr, 15cl; Beamish, The North of England Open Air Museum, County Durham 25b, 26, 29t; Camera Press Ltd 13t, 15b; Robert Harding Picture Library 12, 17t; Holt Studios International cover br, title page t, 4b, 7t, 14t; Hulton Deutsch title page b; Trustees of the Imperial War Museum cover tr, 20t, 21b; Billie Love Historical Collection 27t, 28cl; Peter Millard imprint page, contents page, 4t, 5, 6, 7b, 8tr, 8bl, 8br, 9, 15tl, 22b, 24t, 25t, 29b, 30-31; National Motor Museum, Beaulieu 23b; George Outram Collection 17b, 20b, 27b; Popperfoto cover tl, 19tl; Institute of Agricultural History and Museum of English Rural Life, University of Reading endpapers, 10, 11, 14b, 16, 18, 19b, 21t, 22tr, 24b, 28tr, 28b.